What is "IGHT?"

AN INTERACTIVE BOOK

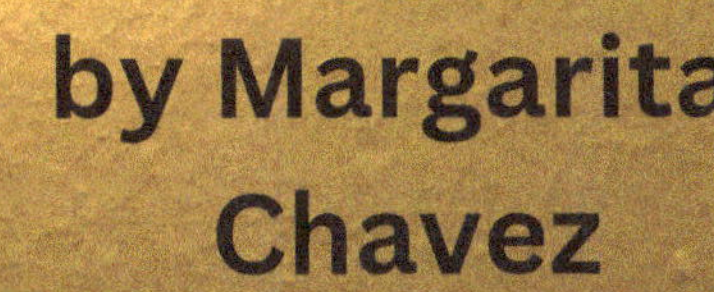

by Margarita Chavez

DEDICATION

This is dedicated to my wonderful son, I am grateful to you for showing me the importance of listening.

Acknowledgment

Elias sat on the floor, pointing with excitement.

"Light!" he said, grinning at the ceiling light.

Mom chuckled. "What a silly sound! What are you trying to say, Elias?" asked his mother.

On a sunny day, Elias reached toward the window.

"Un!" he yelled.

"Say mama," said his mother, but instead he again said "un."

At night, stars twinkled in the dark sky.

Elias stretched his arms.

"Ars!" he said.

Mom smiled and said, "Can you say 'mama'?"

Question: What was Elias trying to say when he said "ars?"

ars?

Elias's eyes widened at the lightning, "ight!" as he pointed.

Mom smiled and asked, "When will you say 'Mama'?"

Question:
What was Elias trying to say when he said "ight?"

Elias and his sister looked at a rainbow and Elias said, "olors!"

Question: What was Elias trying to say when he said "olors? What letter is missing?"

As Elias grew older, his love for light never faded.

He loved switching on lamps, watching fireworks, and staring at glowing candles.

Mom started to see it clearly now.

Elias discovered the art of computer creation, designing them to be transparent and vibrant, decorated with colorful lights.

ELIOSO

"Mom, what was my first word? Elias asked. Was it mom, dad, candy or no?"

"Light or should I say "ight?" said his mother.

Mom hugged him. "And you've always been my bright little star."

Mom?
No?
Candy?
Dad?

QUESTIONS

What was Elias's first word, and why was it special?
Answer: Elias's first word was "ight," which meant "light." It was special because it showed his fascination with all kinds of light, like the sun, lamps, and stars.

What were some of the things Elias pointed to and named in the story?
Answer: Elias pointed to the sun, lamp, light bulb, moon, stars, rainbow, and lightning.

Why didn't Mom realize at first what Elias was saying?
Answer: She thought he was just babbling and didn't connect his words to his love for light. She was also waiting for him to say "mama."

What does Elias's fascination with light teach us about noticing small things in life?
Answer: It shows us the beauty in everyday things and how paying attention to what someone loves can help us understand them better.

Can you name other sources of light that weren't mentioned in the story?
Answer: Examples could include candles, flashlights, fireflies, fireworks, or glow sticks.

www.ingramcontent.com/pod-product-compliance
Lightning Source LLC
Chambersburg PA
CBHW080657160726
PP18578700001B/4